Am I Doing This Right?

Am I Doing This Right?

MEMOIR

Angel King Wilson

Silent Books
Baltimore, MD
2019

For my brother, Earl

unlike all other hyphenated americans
my hyphen is made of blood.
when africa says hello
my mouth is a heartbreak

i don't know how to say hello to my mother.

— Nayyirah Waheed

Baltimore in 8 Words

WATER

I remember in elementary school, after recess, we would form a clumsy line to drink from the water fountain. We breathed heavily, chests against backs, sweat beads dripping down the sides of our faces after hand games, freeze tag, double dutch, and hopscotch. We waited until it was time to put our dry mouths over a small piece of metal and quickly gulped as much water as we could.

One day, DO NOT DRINK signs appeared above the water fountains and large black trash bags covered them. In the bathrooms signs that read HAND WASHING ONLY were posted above the sinks. Water dispensers and white cone cups were placed in the hallways.

It wasn't until I was much older that I learned the water was contaminated with lead. The fountains were built using lead pipes. In the 90s, school officials ordered the water to be tested and metal was found in the water at some schools. The schools with high lead levels had their water turned off. My school, Beechfield Elementary, was one of them. I wonder about the days when all of our young bodies waited to drink the water and why no one came to test our blood and our brains.

I am a teacher at an elementary-middle school and the old water fountains collect dust and balled up gum wrapppers. The students know not to drink from the fountains, but some don't know why. A seventh grader told me that students still drink the water in the bathroom if they are thirsty.

Once I was teaching a Pre-K class and a small girl ran over to the old fountain in the back of the classroom and bent her head to get a drink. I let out a shriek that made her quickly turn around. Although the fountains are turned off, the idea of her drinking the water terrified me.

EDUCATION

"Baltimore The City That Reads" was engraved on the wooden benches across the city. The first time I saw one of the benches I thought to myself, "What do we read?"

In high school, I barely read any of the books that were assigned — *A Raisin in the Sun*, *Catcher in the Rye*, *Of Mice and Men*, Shakespeare plays, and other books that I didn't care to discuss in class. It was nearly impossible to convince me to read the complex and elaborate wording. The opening of *The Scarlet Letter* was the worst. Instead, I read books that interested me like *B-More Careful* about a girl from Baltimore who fell in love with a drug dealer. I remember some girls were excited about *The Coldest Winter Ever*. I'm sure some of us were more interested in the evocative sex scenes, but the storylines were relatable and you didn't have to define every other word.

I attended Western High School — the oldest public all-girl high school in the country and one of the city's top high schools, yet I was failing English with a 35.

But I wasn't the only one. So many girls were failing that the school required certain students to attend English class on Saturdays. About 30 of us sat in a classroom on Saturday mornings just as unenthused as we were during the school week.

Around this time, HBO premiered, *Hard Times at Douglass High: A No Child Left Behind Report Card,* a two-hour long documentary about a high school located in West Baltimore. The statistics showed more than 300 students tested, and most came in at a third, fourth or fifth-grade level.

Now, the wooden benches say, "Baltimore The Greatest City in America."

DEMOCRAT

The vice principal Ms. Almond posted a picture of a white man outside of the main office. He wore a camera-ready smile and a blue suit. Above the picture, on a white sheet of paper she wrote, "If you know the name of the person in this picture, come see Ms. Almond for a prize."

I overheard a student tell Ms. Almond that the man was mayor Martin O'Malley. A few days later, after school, I went to Ms. Almond and told her I knew the man in the picture and she gave me a mini chocolate candy bar.

The adults in my life did not hold conversations about politics. There was never talk about waiting in long lines at the polls on election day. We were convinced that these were the conditions we lived in and they'd stay that way no matter if we voted or not.

The only thing I knew for sure is that we were Democrats. Republicans were rich and white. Democrats were black and poor. I don't know who chose my political status, I fell right into it. I disliked the Republican party without any reasoning. I was a donkey by default.

POVERTY

Poverty is just another word for neglect. There are schools that have more students than they have textbooks and rows of homes without windows and boarded up doors abandoned by the government.

The city is divided into two parts. You can walk down a street and see a hospital surrounded by tall, luxury apartment buildings, but one block down are people living as if Baltimore is a third world country.

In my neighborhood, Asians owned the carry-outs and black boys reigned over the corners and streets. My brothers would take me with them when they went to play dice in the back alley. They'd let me blow the dice for good luck before they shook them around in their hand and rolled.

Some alleyways were cluttered with soda bottles, empty potato chip bags, and candy wrappers. One time I saw a half-filled bottle of A&W crème soda and I wanted to drink it so badly. I picked it up and put it to my lips before someone walked by and we caught eyes. I dropped the bottle and stood there like I had been caught sneaking food out of the refrigerator.

I drank a lot of soda because at that time Sprite would print "Free Sprite" on selected bottle caps. I walked to the store a few times by myself, usually early in the morning and no one knew I was gone. I had used so many of these bottle caps that the Asian man behind the counter told me I wasn't allowed anymore freebies.

On days when we didn't have enough money to buy soda, we drank sugar water. On occasion, we ate white rice with a bit of sugar for dinner, and sometimes cereal with water for breakfast. Once, my sister, my niece and I ate at a homeless shelter. At least that's what I believed it to be because we sat at a wooden table full of strangers and were served a meal on a paper plate. Then, we went home.

And that was the thing about home — somewhere someone wanted to feed you, let you use a phone, sleep on their couch, loan a few dollars, or borrow some sugar.

LIGHTS

If you are in a certain area of Baltimore and the sun is down, you will see blue lights flashing from a tall building or lamp post. I was driving in one of these areas with my friend from West Virginia in my passenger seat.

"What are these blue lights?" Amber tilted her head back to see where the light was coming from.

"Oh, police cameras," I said. Her jaw dropped.

There are 750 cameras across the city. The cameras, also known as CitiWatch, have not decreased crime. For me, they remind me that I am in an unsafe neighborhood.

One summer, I was in a hit and run accident. I was volunteering at the Fresh Food market on Pennsylvania Avenue. When I came outside to pay the meter, my bumper was hanging off and parts of my car were in the street.

I went inside so I could tell the police officer who monitored the market.

"There's a camera out there," she said. "Let me call the office to see if they can run the video back."

Only about 15 minutes had passed before she came and told me they weren't able to see the person who hit my car.

"The cameras rotate. I'm sorry." She was remorseful. She gave me her name and badge number.

I said thank you. The cameras were useless.

REDLINE

Associate professor at Morgan State University, Lawrence Brown coined the terms 'black butterfly' and 'white L'. On the map of Baltimore, the predominately white neighborhoods are located in the center of the city forming an L shape and the black neighborhoods sit on the outskirts of this L, forming the wings of a butterfly.

I met Brown at a panel discussion where we both spoke about the lead poisoning crisis in Baltimore. He argued that the city needed to issue reparations and enter a state of emergency.

But Baltimore has been reluctant to enter a state of emergency because certain issues only affect specified communities. Neighborhoods in the black butterfly experience disproportionate access to housing loans, food desserts, inconvenient bus routes, and archaic school environments.

Although Baltimore began its integration process in 1956, most of the communities are still highly segregated.

I grew up in the black butterfly and there was one white family that lived in my neighborhood. I wondered why they were poor because their white skin made me believe they didn't have to live like us. The other non-black faces I saw were behind the counter at the carry-outs and hair stores.

Money didn't circulate within the black butterfly because black people seldomly owned the businesses in their communities. They rarely could afford to own their homes.

Redlining has kept Baltimore structured so that resources and funding inadequately reach communities. Not only does this structure bring division between neighborhoods and races, but it also robs black Baltimoreans of the opportunity to successfully build a community of their own.

MURALS

There are murals painted across Baltimore at gas stations, on the side of businesses, apartments, and schools. My friend Eric said the art is like a band-aid. When I see a mural, I stare and I decide if it is beautiful.

A mural by artist, Michael Owens is painted on 20 walls across the city. In this mural, black hands are used to form the word LOVE.

Owen said that he uses hands in his art to bring a human element to it, to show people are there.

One of Owen's murals is in my old neighborhood. I'd stop at the red light coming home from work and see the word. It reminds me to stop, look at the scenery. There are more than just buildings here. There are people who make the community.

But I wonder if love has kept them in their community or if they wished to be somewhere more beautiful.

MIGRATION

During the Reconstruction Era, a large number of black people migrated from the South to settle in West Baltimore. My grandparents are from South Carolina. I never had a chance to ask my grandmother about the South; she died before I was old enough to be curious.

I don't know how people leave a place to call another place home.

I take a great sense of pride being from Baltimore, specifically West Baltimore because it tells that I have endured some type of struggle whether it be oppression, poverty, or family dysfunction. I've been to different states and countries, but I think Baltimore is my permanent residence.

After graduating from college, I spent two months in France working at an international language summer camp. When the job ended, I was desperate to be back in Baltimore. I was sick of the tasteless food and the foreign language. Once, I ordered a hot dog and it was wrapped in a thick baguette. I felt like a dog chewing on a toy trying to get to the meat. I wanted to put my feet on Baltimore asphalt and feel the polluted air.

When I drove down North Avenue I was excited to see bunches of black people standing on the streets, vacant homes, and junkies bent over nearly about to fall and hit their face on the concrete. I smiled because I was finally back home.

What's in a Name?

I WAS WITH MY best friend Tamara when we decided to look through the Yellow Pages and call my father.

"What if he answers?" she asked as she handed me the thick yellow book. I opened the book and scrolled my finger down the yellow page. I was looking for the letter C and for the last name Cruz. Joe Cruz. Found it.

"I'm going to call." I picked up the phone receiver and put it to my ear. She watched me as I dialed the numbers. We stared at each other while I listened to the phone ring and ring and ring. No one answered. I left a voicemail. "This is your daughter, please call me back. I found your number in the phone book."

After I hung up the phone I wondered if two middle

schoolers had ruined someone's life. Maybe Joe Cruz had a wife and children, children who needed their father.

No one called back.

I didn't continue the missing person search, so Joe Cruz became this man that I wondered about when I looked in the mirror. I prayed for him before I went to bed. I thought about him when I heard someone call for their father.

When I hear someone say the word Daddy my mind pauses. For that break in time, I remember there is something in life that I missed, a word that I never used in its proper context.

I've only said the word Daddy while having sex.

I wanted love from men just as badly as I wanted love from my father. For me, love was the climax. But what would I be like if Joe Cruz was the first man to kiss my forehead and tell me that he loved me?

The Recipe

IN MY DREAM WORLD, I would have been the child who followed her mother around the kitchen. I'd wait for her to let me whip the eggs or season the chicken. In her kitchen drawer, next to the butter knives, there would have been a little black leather book filled with generations of recipes.

"Milk, two potatoes and an onion," she'd read from the book or call out from off the top of her head. I'd hustle over to the refrigerator or the cabinets repeating the ingredients to myself and then give her what she requested. If she didn't have what she needed, she'd have a substitute. No egg? Use applesauce. No milk? Use water.

I'd ask questions about how much to pour and how many teaspoons of this or that.

We'd talk about the cutest boy in my class while I cut green peppers for chili and we'd laugh at the dress Sister Karen wore to church on Sunday.

· · ·

The clearest childhood memory that I have of my mother is inside of a church. I was four. I cried while the church looked at me out of the corner of their eyes. They clapped their hands and sang the gospel song. My mother picked me up so that I could rest on her shoulder but I kept crying.

I was already attached to my older sister Lisa. I didn't question where my mother had gone, but she arrived on this Sunday to take me with her to church. I was too small to protest, but I didn't want to spend my morning with strangers. Later, I learned that my mother and I lived in seperate homes because she had had a nervous breakdown.

My mother lived in a three bedroom, two story house. Orange medicine bottles lined the corner of her wooden dresser and her bed was made military style. The dim lighting made the room yellow and the walls were white. She shared the house with two old white women. I wondered if they also had had nervous breakdowns.

I thought nervous breakdown was a long way of saying she went crazy. Because she did seem crazy in a quiet way. I wanted to know her thoughts.

. . .

I picture myself following my mother around in the kitchen because for a long time I didn't feel like a woman since I didn't know how to cook. Girls who cooked seemed more fit to have a husband and raise children. I envied girls who knew complicated recipes like stuffed salmon. I wanted to know for myself, but I was too arrogant to ask how and where to start. I blamed my mother.

I wanted to point the finger at my mother, grandmother and great grandmother for not handing down the recipes and teaching me how to be a woman.

I heard that a way to a man's heart was through his stomach and I saw the way women competed after men. I had made up in my mind that there was a connection between womanliness and the ability to cook a meal.

I was casually talking to this guy at work and mid-way

through our conversation he asked if I could cook.

"Fish." I shrugged my shoulders. "I only cook fish."

I didn't cook anything, but I lied because I thought that he was measuring my potential.

I wanted him to check off all of his boxes. Nurturing-check. Nice-check. Discreet-check. Understanding-check. Independent-check. Cook-not quite.

I told myself that I was not yet an adult, not yet a woman until I learned how to cook.

. . .

I wanted my mother to teach me something, something that I could teach my daughter. Fathers taught their sons how to change the car oil, tie a tie, throw a football. But what did women do?

Would she have shown me how to raise children? She had nine. Could she show me how to be a wife?

But life and her nervous breakdown made her silent.

I learned what it meant to be a woman from television, my sisters, the women in my church and the Bible.

In the Book of Proverbs, King Lemuel speaks about a

virtuous woman whose price is far above rubies. Her children call her blessed and her husband praises her. King Lemuel does not mention her name, but names her attributes. She wakes at night to prepare food for her family and she stiches linen and wool for the winter. She makes and sells fine linen. She buys land for her crops and on top of that she gives to the poor. Her lips are the law of kindness.

King Lemuel says that this woman exceeded all the daughters of the land.

I wonder if I could ever reach this level of virtue.

· · ·

If the women in my family have handed down anything, it is their looks. When I was a child, a picture of my grandmother sat on the coffee table. She is wearing a red blouse. Her skin is coffee bean brown, her cheekbones are high and her eyes squinty. Just like mine.

I want to ask her, "Grandma, am I doing this right?"

Peace

ON MONDAY, TUESDAY AND Wednesday I watched snow and rain fall from my bedroom window. It created a white flat mountain with a shiny top layer.

It was Thursday when I got the call from my sister Lisa that Earl died. I wondered if that snow fell on top of my brother. I wondered if he was sleep when his body started to freeze or if the liquor warmed his blood. I wondered about the last person he called. I wondered about the three dollar bills that the police officer said was in his pocket.

And there was that picture of Earl that the officer took of him while he lay there. His arms were folded under his head like a pillow and his eyes were closed. He wore a puffy tan coat and blue denim jeans. The snow under him could have been sand under the sun.

"He looked peaceful," Lisa said about the picture. Peaceful.

The night before the funeral, I stayed up writing because I was expected to say a poem. But I couldn't write a poem for my dead brother that I'd hardly known. I wrote down memories, scratched out lines, read the Bible, wrote more lines.

When I was at the podium, I decided to keep the folded sheet of paper in my back pocket.

"When you have six brothers, sometimes you think they are immortal." I started to cry. I walked back to my seat and used tissues to hide my face. I didn't want to say that I was ashamed to speak about my brother who I hadn't spoken to in three years. My brother who lay in the snow with his cell phone and didn't call me or any of his brothers and sisters. I couldn't let the shame show on my face.

The funeral was over. His casket was closed and we drove in a uniform line to the grave site. The ground was wet because the sun had melted the snow. I sat in the back of the limo and watched the familiar scenery — carry-out, church and liquor store on every block. But on this day, it was depressing. Even the sky was one big cloud, all white and gray. Why did it feel so dreadful yet, so normal?

Dreams

IT WAS THE TYPE of heat that made you tired. I didn't like to use the ceiling fan because the dust clogged my nose. The only air and dim light in the room came from the half-opened window. It was three in the morning and a dream woke me from my sleep.

I dreamed that I was driving down Druid Hill Avenue passing the rounded rusted metal gate that surrounds a body of brown water and patchy grass. My mother was standing on the sidewalk in front of the gate as if she was at a bus stop. She was waving at me to say goodbye. I was waving back. She started to limp her frail body towards my car. Her body was sickly thin and her skeletal wrist sat atop a wooden cane while she pretended to chase after my car.

We smiled and kept waving as I drove away.

I sat up in my bed, tears rolled down my cheeks and drool fell from my mouth. An overwhelming feeling of loss lingered around me.

It made me think of my sophomore year at West Virginia Wesleyan when we studied the psychology of dreams. Sigmund Freud believed dreams derived from desires a person wanted to fulfill. Someone else believed that dreams were feelings a person needed to resolve. There was another belief that dreams were meaningless.

I cried for three days before I decided that God was sending me a warning that I didn't have anymore time to waste on resentment.

. . .

I was in kindergarten when a light skin girl with thick black hair asked me where was my mother. She noticed my sister Lisa was the adult in my life. I told her my mother passed away.

I heard adults use the saying "passed away" so loosely that I thought it meant someone who lived far away.

Distance made me resent her. It wasn't just the physical distance, she felt distant when we were in the same room, especially on holidays. She never bought me a Christmas gift. I thought gifts were the easiest way to express love to a child. I never received a birthday gift either. So, I decided that she didn't love me and she didn't try. But now that I am an adult I realize that she didn't have the love to give.

Maya Angelou said, "I've come to the conclusion that some adults are not really qualified to be parents of young children. They make much better parents of adults. My mother is that type."

My mother is that type too.

Adulthood has brought me an understanding that shows me that *she* needs the love that I had been wanting from her.

I was looking through papers in my desk drawer when I found a letter from my mother. I could hear her talking to me as I read the wrinkled pages. I am attentive to her melodious voice playing in my head.

Towards the end of the letter, I can hear her get emotional. Or maybe it is me. I almost want to skip over the words, but I keep reading.

I'm glad you're doing well. Please forgive me for all those years I missed you growing up — we have lost so many years together — But that doesn't mean I don't love you or care for you. Only God know I would like to spend some time with you if possible. I hope you don't mind — we'll take it slow — we will see one another soon. I'm sorry I wasted all those years not being with you, please forgive me, I really love you and I'm glad you doing fine.
I love you Mommy.

I want to give my mother the chance to love me and I want to return that love to her. I felt this deep, motherly love leave me while she was chasing my car down Druid Hill Avenue.

White Paint

I WAS AT THE Green & Healthy Homes office when I saw a sheet of paper with LEAD POISONING FACT SHEET printed at the top in tall block letters. On the paper it said that if an adult has lead poisoning then their chances of dying are increased by 46 percent.

"What does this mean for me?" I looked at my friend David but I was asking myself.

"Where do they get these numbers?" David stared at the sheet.

I read and reread the words. I folded the paper and placed it in my purse.

I was tested and diagnosed with lead poisoning when I was two years old. I either picked the paint chips off the wall or licked residue off my fingers after crawling around on a dusty floor, I don't know.

But I do remember when I was ten years old, I went for some type of interview where I sat across from a white lady with her brunette hair pulled in a ponytail. She asked me questions from behind her desk. A computer sat to the right side of her and her eyes shifted from my face and then back to the computer screen.

"What are the five oceans on Earth?" she asked. Her head was turned towards me but she kept her fingers on the keyboard of the computer.

"Pacific Ocean… Atlantic Ocean." I looked at her. She looked back at me. I didn't know the other oceans and I didn't recall learning them in school. So, I understood that if I failed this test or whatever it was that it was not any fault of my own.

. . .

In middle school, students were divided according to their level of smartness. Special education and the average classes were placed on the downstairs floor. Upstairs made up the enrichment and advancement academic classes. I was an enrichment student. Advance academic students took Spanish and it seemed they were always one step ahead of us — if we were learning square roots this week, they learned it two weeks ago.

Going into eighth grade, my teachers were discussing if I'd be moved to advance academic, but when the end of the year decisions came back, I was placed in enrichment for the next school year. I went to my math teacher Mr. Butler and asked him why wasn't I moved up.

"Because you're comfortable with getting B's," he shuffled through the papers on his desk.

I didn't study or complete extra credit assignments. I blended in and learned that if I showed up to school, paid attention, and raised my hand that I'd pass my classes.

It was my lackadaisical attitude towards school that affected my education more than lead poisoning.

. . .

I took the fact sheet out of my purse when I got home. Under the words **THE SCARY STATISTICS** was written,

"Any home built before 1978 may contain lead paint; 37.1 million homes contain lead paint."

The home where I lived when I was two years old, 1733 McCulloh Street, is still standing. Three short cement steps sit in front of a white door surrounded by red brick. White curtains hang in the windows of 1733 and the flap of the black mailbox is open. The paint on the door of the house across the street is cracking and chipping like tree bark.

On the street there are broken-down and boarded up homes. Lead poisoning has been able to exist because of neglect.

But we still created a neighborhood from poison, dilapidated homes, and schools that did not teach us enough to pass an IQ test.

We didn't have a chance to choose between lead poisoning and poverty, we were given both.

. . .

"To me having lead poisoning was like having asthma, it just went along with being a black person, in the city, and being poor," my brother Michael said.

Everyone knew someone with lead poisoning.

I didn't attach myself to the stigma. I swept the disease under the rug and I didn't speak about it.

No one spoke about lead poisoning — not parents, teachers, news reporters, doctors.

In elementary school, we drank the water from fountains made with lead pipes. When the water was tested and the results showed a high level of lead, no one made noise about the poisoning of children.

I saw the diagnosis and neglect of lead poisoning as another way to oppress and label poor black people. And it gave us another reason to be helpless and ask for sympathy.

. . .

I met Baltimore based attorney David Albright while we were on a panel for lead poisoning. Albright called me a special case.

"Imagine the things Angel could have done if she didn't have lead poisoning," he said to the host. Maybe he thought I could have been a Harvard graduate, but lead poisoning crippled me.

I was offended because Albright didn't understand that it wasn't just lead poisoning that could have affected me. Maybe it was growing up with neither my mother nor my father, being in classrooms with more than 30 children, catching two buses to school every morning, not being able to buy uniforms and new shoes, or never knowing what I was going to eat for dinner. But I stayed quiet.

Albright went on to say that 99.9 percent of their clients are born into poverty. I thought about the brown faces of children whose life options are cut in half.

This came to my mind while I was reading the fact sheet that told me I could possibly die earlier then everyone else. But, everyone knows that people who live in poverty have a greater chance of dying young.

I separated myself from lead poisoning and poverty — the effects, the stereotypes, the labels. I crumbled the paper and threw it in the trash.

This May or May Not Be True

My mother called me and said that she saw my father at church. He said, "I want my daughter."

I should have asked if she took down his number, but I held the phone receiver against my ear and let her talk.

I was jealous because she had seen him and I had never laid eyes on the man. And he had said that he wanted me, but I was stuck with the other parent.

Her call woke me out of my sleep. Maybe it was a dream. I was 12 years old.

If it wasn't a dream, I think it was my mother's guilt that made her pick up the phone and call me. I've always been curious about my father, but I didn't know what questions to ask. Maybe she was trying to ease my mind from thinking she did not know who or where he was.

My sister Kiesha told me to let it go because she didn't know her father either. But Kiesha and I were different. Kiesha had always loved our mother more than I thought she deserved. I couldn't honestly love a woman who held a secret that belonged to me. I wanted to know my father.

Is it easier for men to forget? Do they think about their child when the hours are slow at the office or when they see children playing outside?

I don't think the children ever forget.

Man Down

MY MOTHER WAS WARNING me about the women in our family when she told me that my grandmother use to say, "I will die with a man in my arms."

"Learn from my mistakes, don't be like me," my mother pleaded. She talked about her regrets and the women in my family — women who chased after men and were nothing more than mothers.

Against her premonition, my grandmother died in her small home all by her lonesome. My aunt found her on the floor after she had a stroke. That's what my cousin Renee told me.

I also heard she died of cancer. My mother said she had to get one of her breasts cut off.

But I never heard that she died with a man in her arms.

A Conversation about a Man

"YOU OWE IT TO me," I was standing in the kitchen using my shoulder to hold my phone against my ear while I washed the dishes.

"Well I don't want to talk about it over the phone," my mother let out a sigh.

A week later we drank Coca-Cola while she talked to me about men. Relationship advice was her favorite. "So, how's Eric?" she asked, then smiled with her eyes. We talked about my boyfriend, then watched fragments of the news.

When it was silent I said, "So you wanna talk about my father." She sat up straight in her seat and placed the palm of her hands on her legs.

"I lived on 1733 McCulloh Street," she said as she rubbed her thighs.

My father would bring her ice cream. He worked at the Friendly's downtown. In my mind, I can see my mother sitting on the marble steps of our house, waiting for Mr. Man to bring her some melted ice cream, maybe her favorite — mint chocolate chip. When he showed up, she'd be unconcerned about the whereabouts of her children, licking her ice cream off the spoon, smiling to show her big white teeth, and laughing her high-pitched laugh. Then, they'd sneak off and have sex before one of the children got back from wherever.

"I use to call him Ted, yeah, that's what I use to call him, Ted," she nodded her head. It looked like an interrogation. She sat at the dining room table and I sat across from her.

"What was his real name?" I asked.

"I don't know his real name. T-E-D, that's how he spell it." She spelled it to fill the space of not knowing his last name.

"He told me he was making a hundred dollas a week

at Friendly's, so I thought I'd work there too. By the time I got the job, he moved on to another job." She sat there, upright in her seat with her hands on her thighs. "I was pregnant when I got the job," she said.

"So what about," I paused, "why does Lisa say my father worked with the carnival?"

For most of my life, I figured my father went to the next city with the carnival because no one had ever seen him again or spoke about him.

"He had odd jobs. He was always doing this and that. When I first met him, he worked at the carnival. When I seen him again, he was working at Friendly's." She sipped her Coca-Cola.

"So whose Joe Cruz?" I asked.

"Joe Cruz was a friend I use to know, I had some male friends, but I know definitely Ted was your father."

"Did you think Joe Cruz was my father?"

"Joe Cruz like a *Mexican*."

"Why'd you'd put his name on my birth certificate?"

"Did I do that?" her words started to jumble together.

"Oh wow what was I thinking?"

"I don't know," I answered her rhetorical question. I felt like it needed an answer.

"I just put anything really. But Ted is your father."

I sat across from her and didn't say a word.

"Sorry about that Angel, it's so embarrassing," her voice muffled behind her tears. "I just want you to do better. You going with this man and that man and you may think you can't get pregnant, but every time I would lay down with a man, God would tell on me. Sin will catch up to you."

I was catching up to her. I wouldn't let her forget her past and I nagged her for answers. But after she poured her honesty, I felt a new love between us.

Still, I wanted to cry. The need to know my father didn't disappear, but the reality of knowing him seemed just as far as it was when I walked into my mom's apartment. I want to see his face. I want to hear his voice. I want to know his side of the story.

Genes

MY COUSIN BRENDA TOLD me that my great grandmother was Indian Cherokee and her hair fell down her back.

It made me think about the time when I was brushing my mother's silky shoulder-length hair. She was sitting on the couch and I was standing behind her. Our neighbors gave me her name — Lil' Annette. They'd call me her twin.

But I couldn't see the resemblance. I was darker than her honey freckled skin and my hair was thick and stiff in my ponytails.

I desperately wanted long hair, but the gene skipped me somewhere in the mix between Indian and African, the African gene was more dominant. And because of that, I am called African American. I am black.

There is nothing left that ties me to the side of me that is Indian Cherokee. I wonder if I let my hair grow long, would I look more like my ancestors.

Hair Gods

Ponytails

My sister Lisa parts my hair into four sections, slaps Blue Magic hair grease in the palm of her hand and rubs the grease on my scalp. She dips the rough bristle brush in a cup of water, strokes my bushy hair into four tight pony-tails — two in the front right above my ears and two in the back. I stand on the step stool in the bathroom and stare at my wide, shiny forehead and puffy ponytails. I think I look pretty.

Perm

I wanted to look like the girls on the front of boxed perms with their shiny curls, straight ponytails, and bangs. I was in the seventh grade when my sister permed my hair. She smeared a thick layer of Vaseline on my hairline and scalp, a process called basing, to protect the perm from burning my skin. With gloves on, she applied the white cream to my hair. The smell reeked of rotten eggs. After I felt a burning sensation, we rushed to the kitchen sink to rinse. Under the faucet water, I smelled the chemicals being washed from my head. I felt her touch my scalp as she ran her fingers through my stringy, wet hair.

She dried my hair with a towel. I turned to look at my side profile in the mirror and I slowly stroked my hair.

Weave

I'd show my hair stylist a picture and she'd give me drop curls, bob, middle part weave, side part weave, invisible part, whatever I asked.

My stylist would gel most of my hair into two braids, leaving a section of my natural hair out at the top of my head. Afterward, I'd sit under a dryer for an hour, sometimes longer and wait for the gel to harden like dried paste.

I'd then go sit in the stylist chair where she measured the track against my head horizontally, cut and glued it to my hard gelled hair. This process was repeated several times until the hair was covered. My natural hair at the top of my head was flat ironed so that all the straightness blended together. And there I am, a new woman.

Locs

The history of locs date back to ancient times. Carvings of Egyptians Pharaohs with locs have been found on tombs and mummified bodies were discovered with their locs still intact.

In 1999, a Levi's ad portrayed an African American man with locs, holding a sign that said, "Conformity leads to Mediocrity."

I picture myself, in my old age with gray dreads that exude wisdom and survival.

Short Cut

I thought I'd go ahead and give my real hair a try. Real, not natural — I still needed a perm to achieve that straight sporty short hairstyle. I knew I'd look nice in the style because I had recently had a short cut with fake hair. My boyfriend at the time liked the short fake hair, so I thought why not.

The back and sides of my hair were cut close to my scalp and my bangs fell above my eyebrows. I received compliments on how well the style fit my face. I loved being able to scratch my scalp and wear my own hair, but after putting heat to my head every other day to maintain the style, my hair started to break off. My bangs in the front were shorter and my hair was closer to my scalp. The style was sheered and sleek on the first day out of the salon, but any day after that was a struggle to get the same look.

Braids

I wear braids so that my hair can return to its natural state — the thick curly dry texture that stood on my head before I had my first perm. When I wear braids I feel closer to my roots.

A Debate

"When a woman changes her hair drastically all the time, a man can see she doesn't know herself," my boyfriend said to me from his end of the table.

"Women, well, black women, like to express themselves. It's nothing wrong with that," I said.

"You can change your hair. But why bangs one week and long red hair the next. Like your friend, Asia."

"It's like changing your nails. Some men like it. You can't speak for all men."

"Hmph," he continued, "Just pick a hairstyle. You can change it up, but pick a style."

"You can't put women in a box." I am adamant, but silently a part of me agrees with him.

Growth

In an interview, Nigerian novelist Chimamanda Ngozi Adichie was asked if her dramatic change in hairstyles had something to do with her creative process as a writer.

She answered, "No, it says a lot more about where I am

in my growth process as a woman."

Sometimes, I still feel the need to straighten my hair for certain occasions because braids or puffy styles aren't seen as professional. Other times, I feel the pressure of non-conformity when all I want is a new look.

Every woman of every complexion should want to look in the mirror, stripped of make-up, wearing their natural hair and see themselves as beautiful.

I, like Adichie, am still growing.

Sow a Seed

IF THERE WAS A mall fountain, I'd ask for a quarter so that I could close my eyes, make a wish and throw the coin in the wavy water. I'd stare at the coins and wonder about the amount of money swimming at the bottom.

Every time I'd wish for thousands of dollars. I was sure wealth would come to me as an adult because my life would be in my own hands.

Once, I was talking with my friend Kevin about growing up in Baltimore.

"How did you know you were poor?" Kevin asked. "I just thought everyone around me was living the same way."

I'd never thought about how I discovered the level of classes and when I figured out that I was on the bottom tier. Maybe it was TV. Probably the Disney Channel. Or maybe it was because I had a pair of shoes that were a size too big, so I had to stuff socks into the toe.

I always had a feeling that there was greener grass somewhere, but I couldn't see it.

There was a time when I was playing in the mud in our backyard and I decided to bury a dollar that was in my back pocket. I was digging and patting the mud on top of my single dollar bill when my sister Lisa walked through the back door to ask what was I doing.

"I'm burying my money. Pastor said you'll get your money back," I told her.

The night before at Bible study, Pastor Barnes preached about sowing a seed in church so God could bless you with more money. I was in and out of sleep. The church kept repeating, Seed Bring Back My Money. I caught part of the sermon while I was awake and thought I, a five year old girl, had found her millionaire miracle.

Lisa laughed and kept laughing.

It took me much longer to understand the concept of

giving money to the church to earn it back because even though we were a spiritual family, we were poor.

I didn't think being poor bothered most of the people I knew, because in the Bible, the poor are favored by Jesus. All of my prayers included a "thank you for the clothes on my back, roof over my head, food on the table and shoes on my feet. Amen."

Still, I was looking for the balance between gratefulness and greed. It confused me how we could serve a God who made the world, but we relied on food stamps and first of the month checks.

I learned something from my elders that they didn't seem to understand themselves — God did not send things that you didn't work for. He didn't care about for the wishes I made at the mall fountain to become a wealthy woman.

But there is a young girl inside of me that would be heartbroken if she discovered that all those quarters were wasted and they could've gone to her savings.

Colophon

The text of this book is set in Baskerville Regular, a typeface designed by John Baskerville in 1757.
Headings are set in Georgia Bold, designed by Matthew Carter in 1993.

Front Cover is set in Euphemia UCAS & Georgia Regular. Euphemia was designed by Ross Mills in 2006.
Back Cover is set in Georgia Regular. Spine is set in Euphemia UCAS.

Cover design and illustration by Angel King Wilson.

Made in the USA
Coppell, TX
30 July 2021

59718816R00049